John
Wayne

From
Western Hero
to
Hollywood
Legend

Contents

JOHN WAYNE

First published in the UK in 2012 by Instinctive Product Development

© Instinctive Product Development 2012

www.instinctivepd.com

Printed in China

ISBN: 978-1-908816-44-3

Designed by: BrainWave

Creative Director: Kevin Gardner

Written by: Jessica Bailey

Images courtesy of PA Photos, Shutterstock and Wiki Commons

■ **BELOW:** John Wayne is seen on hosreback during the filming of the western *The Big Trail*, in 1930.

Chapter 1:
The Duke on Screen

John Wayne holds the record for the most leading roles – 142 – by an actor, but his beginnings on the silver screen were somewhat more humble. He first appeared on screen in 1926 in *The Great K & A Train Robbery* as an un-credited extra and prop boy in this stunt-driven film, directed by Lewis Seiler, starring Tom Mix. Based on the book by Paul Leicester Ford, the movie was filmed on location in Royal Gorge, Colorado and was highly rated – particularly for Mix's fine performance as an undercover detective trying to infiltrate a gang of train robbers – with both audiences and critics alike. This fast-paced Western with its romance and triumph of good over evil, gave Wayne a taste of life in film and, despite his academic and sporting achievements, it was the movies that would eventually win his heart and soul.

■ **BELOW: American actor Tom Mix at the Longchamp Racecourse in Paris in 1925.**

The first "talkie" to use sound on film technology was *The Jazz Singer*, released in October 1927, but developments had been underway to synchronise sound with image since the early 1900s. By the time *Men Without Women* was released in 1930, talkies were fast becoming a global phenomenon and the drawl with which cinema audiences would become more than accustomed could be heard in a small part when the "Duke" played a radio operator in John Ford's undersea war adventure. The film features a mixture of talking sequences, silent passages and inter-titles, and while the profits of more than $2.6 million for Al Jolson's performance in *The Jazz Singer* had convinced the four largest studios in Hollywood that the new technology was worth investing in, there were still huge developments to be made; production facilities and theatres

needed to be converted to allow for sound films. All this took time and while Warner Bros began to rake in the profits with their first talkie in 1927 and the three that followed, the other studios began to quicken the pace of their own conversions.

Most movie theatres, particularly those outside of larger urban areas, were not equipped to show films with sound and, despite increased profits, the major studios were still not convinced of the talkies' appeal. However, by the mid-1930s, just 10 years after Wayne made his first screen appearance, they were beginning to realise the benefits of the advanced technology and the Duke himself found a niche with his all-American persona and voice at a time when many of the silent movie stars were beginning to wane in popularity when it was discovered that their voices just

■ **ABOVE:** Al Jolson performs in blackface makeup in the 1927 movie *The Jazz Singer*.

didn't fit the profile required to make it "big" in Hollywood's soon-to-come Golden Age.

When Wayne carried out the role of the radio operator in this 1930 film starring Frank Albertson, it saw the story begin after a brief shore leave in Singapore for the crew of a US Navy S-13 submarine. It was an opportunity for the sailors to quench their thirst for liquor and women, but the fun wasn't to last, and all men were ordered back on duty so that the vessel could make it to safer waters before a storm hit the coastline. Many of the crew are still drunk when the storm swirls towards the submarine and vital radio equipment is knocked out of action. The crew begin to send distress signals, but with a limited amount of oxygen on board, tempers soon flare and arguments are rife, as the men begin to panic about whether any of them will survive if they aren't rescued. With mounting tension between two leading characters, torpedo launcher Burke (played by Kenneth MacKenna) and ship commander, Weymouth (Charles K Gerrard), the stress of the situation grows through the drama.

■ **BELOW:** Movie director John Ford posing on a yacht.

Men Without Women (1930)
– first motion picture with credit

FACTS

Released:	31 January 1930
Directed by:	John Ford
Produced by:	John Ford
Written by:	John Ford, James Kevin McGuinness
Starring:	Frank Albertson, Kenneth MacKenna, Charles K Gerrard
Music by:	Carli Elinor
Distributed by:	Fox Film Corporation

Stagecoach (1939)
– stardom beckons

FACTS

Released:	15 February 1939
Directed by:	John Ford
Produced by:	Walter Wanger
Written by:	Ernest Haycox
Screenplay by:	Dudley Nichols, Ben Hecht
Starring:	Claire Trevor, John Wayne, Thomas Mitchell, John Carradine, Andy Devine, George Bancroft
Music by:	Gerard Carbonara
Distributed by:	United Artists

Westerns had been becoming popular in Hollywood for some time before this film in the late-1930s; however, *Stagecoach* was to influence the way this film genre was portrayed and perceived for many movies to come. There is a good mix of characters in the film from Dallas (played by Trevor) a scandalous woman who has been driven out of town, to The Ringo Kid, a fugitive played by Wayne, to a pregnant Lucy Mallory, (played by Louise Platt) the wife of a cavalry officer who is taking the stagecoach to be reunited with her husband. The journey begins in Tonto, Arizona destined for Lordsburg in New Mexico, but the passengers know they are not going to find the going easy.

Directed by John Ford, this Western is a solid portrayal of life in the late 1880s in the days of white man's conflict with Native Americans. The screenplay is an adaptation of a short story by Haycox written in 1937, *The Stage to Lordsburg*, where the characters take the stagecoach through dangerous Apache territory. Filmed on location in Monument Valley on the Arizona/ Utah border, the movie was to bring about Wayne's rise to fame from B-rated Western actor to star, and set the scene for further Westerns directed by John Ford who cleverly combined shots of the Valley with Iverson Movie Ranch in California and other location backdrops. The formula for this movie has remained unchanged and no director since has ever improved upon it according to many critics.

■ **ABOVE: John Wayne and actress Claire Trevor in a scene from the 1939 movie *Stagecoach*.**

■ **ABOVE: Albert Adams (centre), who was wounded when fighting the Japanese, looks on as John Wayne autographs his cast at a New Guinea hospital station.**

War films released in the mid- to late-1930s and the 1940s were undoubtedly concerned with propaganda, and this movie, directed by David Miller, proves no exception. Keen to make a strong point about Japanese atrocities during the Second World War (1939-1945), *Flying Tigers* was significant for Wayne's career as he made the transition from the genre of the Western to that of war. At the time, close-ups of the enemy dying with blood pouring from his mouth and Wayne's shots where he determinedly goes "in for the kill" must have

been reassuring to US and allied audiences the world over, even though today, these crazed scenes may seem a little over the top. There was great turbulence globally and an all-action American hero such as Wayne must surely have provided some comfort during extreme times.

Filming of the black-and-white movie took place between May and July 1942 starring Wayne as a mercenary fighter pilot fighting the Japanese in China prior to the United States joining the Second World War. The legendary Flying Tigers were

a military unit unsanctioned by the US government at the time and missions were death-defying and hazardous. Wayne plays the character of sensitive commander, Jim Gordon, who along with John Carroll, playing reckless Woody Jason, set out on dangerous missions motivated by the bounty they receive for every enemy aircraft shot down. The crew of the Curtiss P-40 are an eclectic mix of men where some are interested in the actual combat while others are true patriots. Carroll's character is a troublemaker unused to teamwork

Flying Tigers (1942)

FACTS

Released:	8 October 1942
Directed by:	David Miller
Produced by:	Edmund Grainger
Written by:	Kenneth Gamet, Barry Trivers
Starring:	John Wayne, John Carroll, Anna Lee
Music by:	Victor Young
Distributed by:	Republic Pictures

who endangers the lives of his fellow crew. Meanwhile, he begins a romance with Red Cross worker Brooke Elliot (Anna Lee) who actually has her eye on Jim Gordon. Jason takes the young woman out on a date and ends up late for patrol. As a result, Hap Smith (who has been grounded for his failing eyesight), takes his place without permission and ends up dying in a collision with a Japanese fighter. Following the death of Blackie Bales earlier in the film, this proves the final straw for Gordon, who fires his old friend on Sunday 7 December 1941 – the day that the Japanese launched their devastating attack on Pearl Harbor. Despite being sacked, Woody Jason secretly boards a plane when Gordon flies solo on a daring mission to bomb a bridge carrying a supply train. When their plane is hit, having missed the train, Gordon bails out, but Woody, who has been shot, deliberately flies into the train.

Two Flying Tigers, Lawrence Moore and Kenneth Sanger, were technical advisors for the film, although none of the actual American Volunteer Group (AVA) were mentioned in the movie by name.

■ **BELOW: Two actual P-40 fighter planes, painted with the shark-face emblem of the famed "Flying Tigers," are seen standing in line on the airfield.**

Red River (1948)

FACTS

Released:	30 September 1948
Directed by:	Howard Hawks, (Arthur Rosson, co-director)
Produced by:	Howard Hawks
Written by:	Borden Chase
Screenplay by:	Charles Schnee
Starring:	John Wayne, Montgomery Clift, Walter Brennan, Joanne Dru, John Ireland
Music by:	Dimitri Tiomkin
Distributed by:	United Artists

Red River received huge critical acclaim for its fictional portrayal of the first cattle drive from Texas to Kansas (based on the opening of the Chisholm Trail in 1867). The film is considered by many to be one of the best 10 Westerns ever made. The movie, directed by Howard Hawks (his first Western), is a classic yet complex tale spanning 15 years of rivalry and rebellion, where the director shows his versatility as a filmmaker in one of his most extravagant and ambitious films. Costs amounted to more than $3 million, which took it over

budget; however, it went on to be a top-grossing film in the year it was released. Shot on location in Arizona and Mexico, the story concentrates on Tom Dunson, a ruthless, contemptible cattleman desperate to set up a cattle ranch in Texas. The epic story was the first of five films that Wayne would work on with Hawks and saw one of the Duke's best performances. The film received two Academy Award nominations for the film editing and the story. It probably missed out on other nominations because of the genre, however, critics believe

■ **TOP:** John Wayne and Montgomery Clift in the western classic *Red River*.

■ **ABOVE:** John Wayne presents a special Oscar to veteran film director Howard Hawks, during the 47th Annual Academy Awards ceremony in 1975.

that Wayne, Montgomery Clift (who plays Wayne's adopted son), Hawks and score composer Tiomkin should all have been in the running.

The plot concentrates on a time just after the American Civil War (1861-1865), when respected veteran, Captain Kirby York (Wayne), is expected to take up the role of commander at Fort Apache, a remote cavalry post. The command of his own regiment had, by this time, been given to Lieutenant Colonel Owen Thursday (played by Fonda), despite his lacking experience with the Native Americans he is expected to oversee. When there is unrest among the Indians, Thursday ignores advice from York to treat them with honour and respect, and persistent problems lead to rebellion. Thursday leads the troops into battle in the hills – a veritable suicide mission – and few men make it back. The film was the first of Ford's "Cavalry Trilogy"; *She Wore A Yellow Ribbon* (1949) and *Rio Grande* (1950) followed, based loosely on Custer and the Battle of Little Bighorn. It was one of the first movies to show a sympathetic approach to Native Americans and definitely one of the first to have some authenticity, while critics praise the friction between Wayne's and Fonda's characters. Filmed in black-and-white in Monument Valley, Arizona, the backdrop for the movie is breathtaking and Wayne is true to his image as the archetypal cowboy – tough and daring, yet compassionate and sensitive.

■ **RIGHT: Shirley Temple.**

Fort Apache (1948)

FACTS

Released:	9 March 1948
Directed by:	John Ford
Produced by:	Merian C Cooper, John Ford
Written by:	James Warner Bellah
Screenplay by:	Frank S Nugent
Starring:	John Wayne, Henry Fonda, Shirley Temple
Music by:	Richard Hageman
Distributed by:	RKO

■ **ABOVE:** The Post Headquarters building where Nathan Brittles (John Wayne) lived in the movie *She Wore A Yellow Ribbon*, located at Goulding's Lodge near Monument Valley, USA.

Wayne plays Captain Nathan Brittles, a cavalry officer stationed in the South West, just one campaign away from retirement. While rallying his troops for combat against the Cheyenne, he is ordered to escort the wife and niece of his commanding officer to the stage line at Sudros Wells. Joanne Dru – who plays Major Mac Allshard's niece, Olivia – finds herself attracting the attention of several soldiers, while Wayne's portrayal of an older man reluctantly moving away from his life in the military is sensitive and commanding. The second of director Ford's trilogy, the film was one of the most expensive Westerns of its time. It met with critical acclaim and is still one of the most popular classics today. Filmed in colour – many feel that Ford should have moved away from black-and-white more often – Monument Valley on the edge of Arizona was chosen as the location for its stunning backdrop and imposing scenery. Winton Hoch won the Academy Award in 1950 for Best Color Cinematography.

■ **ABOVE:** A scene from *She Wore A Yellow Ribbon*.

■ **BELOW:** Joanne Dru and her husband, actor John Ireland, arrive for the Academy Awards presentations in Hollywood, 1950.

She Wore A Yellow Ribbon (1949)

FACTS

Released:	22 October 1949
Directed by:	John Ford
Produced by:	Merian C Cooper, Lowell J Farrell, John Ford
Written by:	James Warner Bellah
Screenplay by:	Frank S Nugent, Laurence Stallings
Starring:	John Wayne, Joanne Dru, John Agar, Victor McLaglen, Ben Johnson, Harry Carey Jr
Music by:	Richard Hageman
Distributed by:	RKO

Producer, Edmund Grainger, was blessed when his father backed his plan for an epic war movie based on the Marines' assault on Iwo Jima during the Second World War. Head of studio, Herbert Yates, was unconvinced by a big budget production, but changed his mind when head of sales, Jim Grainger, promised him that his son's idea would be resoundingly successful with a great director and a big star. Dwan was quickly brought on board and Wayne was chosen for the leading role.

The film was granted a bigger budget than most Republic pictures (around $1 million), but even that would have greatly increased without the co-operation and input of the Marines who were brought in to make soldiers out of the men playing the parts. The film went on to make huge profits (grossing more than $5 million in the US and Canada) and became one of the most popular films of 1950. It also turned Wayne into a huge

movie star and saw him, for the first time, billed as one of the 10 most popular stars in the United States. It was, according to many, his best war movie and he was rewarded with his first Academy Award nomination for Best Actor. He also won praise from the US military for his convincing portrayal of a Marine.

Sands Of Iwo Jima (1949)

FACTS

Released:	14 December 1949
Directed by:	Allan Dwan
Produced by:	Edmund Grainger
Written by:	Harry Brown, James Edward Grant
Starring:	John Wayne, John Agar, Forrest Tucker, Adele Mara
Music by:	Victor Young
Distributed by:	Republic Pictures

■ **RIGHT:** Makeup man Dan Greenway gets three heroes of the actual Iwo Jima flag-raising ready for the cameras filming *Sands of Iwo Jima*.

■ **BELOW:** The flag-raising scene on Iwo Jima, from *Sands of Iwo Jima*.

The on-screen chemistry between Wayne and Maureen O'Hara was unique with their (often) love/hate relationship; however, they always showed each other respect. *Rio Grande* showcased this chemistry and charm more than any other film in which both actors were present. Ford concentrates perhaps a little too much on the songs within the film (many critics felt the musical inclusions slowed the picture down), but there is also a great deal of humour, friction and fighting to ensure that the movie is a legendary Western. Wayne portrays a cavalry colonel who finds his estranged son, Jefferson "Jeff" Yorke (played by Jarman) enlisted in his regiment. Kathleen Yorke (O'Hara) turns up to get their underage son out of service and the warring couple find that they are still very much in love, though neither will admit it. Wayne and O'Hara are particularly good at building the tension and the film speeds up during the second half. Herbert Yates had allowed Ford to make *The Quiet Man* starring Wayne and insisted that the two men – along with O'Hara – make *Rio Grande* in order to recoup the losses he expected. The head of Republic Pictures must have been pleasantly surprised when both films became huge hits.

■ **BELOW:** John Wayne is shown on horseback in a scene from *Rio Grande* on location.

Rio Grande (1950)

FACTS

Released:	15 November 1950
Directed by:	John Ford
Produced by:	Merian C Cooper, John Ford
Written by:	James Warner Bellah
Screenplay by:	James K McGuinness
Starring:	John Wayne, Maureen O'Hara, Ben Johnson, Claude Jarman Jr
Music by:	Victor Young
Distributed by:	Republic Pictures

This Western is based on *The Searchers* by Alan Le May, published in 1954 covering the Texas-Indian wars, and proved a commercial success for Warner Bros. Its success didn't end there when it was given 12th place on the American Film Institute's list in 2007 of the Top 100 Great Movies of all time, and the following year was named the Greatest American Western of all time. For director, Ford, it is perhaps one of his (nowadays) most admired and influential films, shot on location in Monument Valley. At the time of the film's release, however, it was misunderstood by its critics who left it unappreciated and basically unrecognised. The story is an emotionally complex tale of a dangerous, hate-ridden quest of self-discovery following a Comanche massacre. In true John Ford style, the film is a social commentary about racial prejudice and sexism at a time when hard-nosed independent men found it difficult to examine their own psychological turmoil. Natalie Wood plays one of Wayne's nieces who have been abducted by Native Americans. The Duke plays a bigot and a racist hell-bent on finding his family. A lonely man in an anti-heroic role, this characterisation was undoubtedly one of Wayne's best performances.

The Searchers (1956)

FACTS

Released:	13 March 1956
Directed by:	John Ford
Produced by:	Cornelius Vanderbilt Whitney
Written by:	Alan Le May
Screenplay by:	Frank S Nugent
Starring:	John Wayne, Jeffrey Hunter, Vera Miles, Ward Bond, Natalie Wood
Music by:	Max Steiner, (title song by Stan Jones)
Distributed by:	Warner Bros

■ **BELOW:** Natalie Wood.

Rio Bravo (1959)

FACTS

Released:	18 March 1959
Directed by:	Howard Hawks
Produced by:	Howard Hawks
Written by:	B H McCampbell, Jules Furthman, Leigh Brackett
Starring:	John Wayne, Dean Martin, Ricky Nelson, Angie Dickinson, Walter Brennan, Ward Bond, John Russell
Music by:	Dimitri Tiomkin
Distributed by:	Warner Bros

This 1959 Western is considered a masterpiece of American cinema, which not only starred Wayne, but had a high-profile supporting cast as well. Many believe that despite Hawks' genius, the cast are what actually make this movie special. It is regarded as one of the director's best, with just four close-up shots, a long opening scene with no dialogue, and an outstanding score, including the hauntingly ominous *El Deguello* theme by Tiomkin. With Dean Martin and Nelson – a fifties teen-idol – in the cast, it is no surprise that the film contains three songs. The motion picture was made in response to Carl Foreman's *High Noon* because Hawks and Wayne disliked it. Foreman had been out of the Communist Party for around 10 years at the time of writing, but he was still called before the House Un-American Activities Committee (HUAC) where he declined to name names and was branded uncooperative.

Wayne was instrumental in hounding Foreman out of the US for which he had no regrets. *High Noon* went on to become highly respected despite its earlier troubles and it has been a favourite of many American Presidents. Wayne's objection was that it was an allegory for blacklisting which he actively supported. He considered the film un-American. *Rio Bravo* was a conservative response.

The Alamo (1960)

FACTS

Released:	24 October 1960
Directed by:	John Wayne
Produced by:	John Wayne
Written by:	James Edward Grant
Starring:	John Wayne, Richard Widmark, Laurence Harvey
Music by:	Dimitri Tiomkin
Distributed by:	United Artists

■ **RIGHT:** The main entrance to the Alamo in San Antonio, Texas.

■ **BELOW:** John Wayne directs a scene for the Hollywood movie *The Alamo* with the Todd A-O camera.

■ **BELOW RIGHT:** Lajean Ethridge, 27, (centre) alongside John Wayne, was stabbed to death at a house near *The Alamo* film site on 11 October 1959. Chester Harvey Smith, 32, a movie extra was charged with murder.

It's well documented that Wayne was obsessed with the 1836 Battle of the Alamo and this motion picture was his sterling attempt to recreate events. The film became a historical epic starring Wayne as Davy Crockett, which also featured Frankie Avalon, Patrick Wayne, Ken Curtis, Hank Worden, Linda Cristal and Denver Pyle. Some felt that Wayne wanted to make a political statement and that this movie was the vehicle he chose to do just that; he was outspoken and an active supporter of Nixon and politics were an important part of Hollywood at the time. *The Alamo* was the most expensive film made in 1960 and although it faired well at the box office, it didn't make enough to recoup its costs. By this time, Wayne was suffering from lung cancer and his health began to deteriorate during filming.

It had taken a huge strain on Wayne, both physically and financially, and he'd had to fight the studio to prove he could be a good director after 30 years on the other side of the camera. That was a blow for the Hollywood legend who had dreamed about making this film for decades. While many believe he made the film for political reasons, some claim that the true motivation for the film was the story of Alamo itself and the heroics of the men that went into battle there fighting for the basic cause of freedom. Whatever his reasons for making the movie, Wayne was clearly influenced by Ford's earlier directions including structuring the film along the same lines as Westerns, providing characters for comic relief and anecdotal scenes. But many believe that this film doesn't work because of Wayne being in the movie himself. People love John Wayne movies, but here as Davy Crockett, he perhaps comes across as, well, John Wayne. He had declined to act in the movie, but without his appearance it was feared that the movie would make little or no money at all. Wayne had no choice but to act. He was also not overly rated as a director. Wayne was a larger-than-life American who understood good American values. Whether he could deviate from being John Wayne – either in character or on the other side of the camera – was possibly questionable and critical response was mixed.

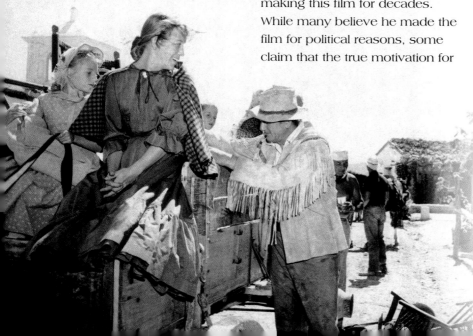

The Longest Day (1962)

FACTS

Released:	4 October 1962 (released in France in September 1962)
Directed by:	Ken Annakin (British and French), Andrew Marton (US), Bernhard Wicki (German), Gerd Oswald (parachute drop), Darryl F Zanuck (uncredited)
Produced by:	Darryl F Zanuck
Written by:	Cornelius Ryan
Screenplay by:	Romain Gary, James Jones, David Pursall, Cornelius Ryan, Jack Seddon
Starring:	John Wayne, Sean Connery, Henry Fonda, Robert Mitchum, Richard Burton, Peter Lawford, Rod Steiger, Kenneth More, Irina Demick, Robert Wagner
Music by:	Maurice Jarre
Distributed by:	20th Century Fox

■ **RIGHT INSET:** John Wayne in a scene from *The Longest Day*.

■ **RIGHT:** Three wartime Spitfires in flight, used in the filming of *The Longest Day*. These three Spitfires were found with the Belgian Air Force, being used for target practice. They were fitted with new engines and repainted in new colours.

This epic Second World War movie was Zanuck's bid to put Fox back in the limelight with him in control following his demise at the studio and the commercial failure of *Cleopatra*. This accurate depiction of the D-Day landings on 6 June 1944 was widely appreciated by war veterans almost 20 years later, which helped to secure its producer's future. Zanuck had become known for his European collaborations, and four separate filming units were employed for the black-and-white movie, which enabled speed and economy. The film covers many different viewpoints of the landings, from British glider troops who captured inland bridges, to the boats approaching Normandy, and the harrowing amphibious assaults that ensued. The film also portrays the shock of the German high command as they are caught unawares, and the panic of their defending soldiers.

The movie is action-packed with complex scenes, which touch the emotions of the audience, including the scene on Omaha beach where a line of soldiers sacrificed their lives, and the re-enactment of an entire battalion being dropped onto a German stronghold where the enemy is very much awake. German director, Wicki, was particularly praised for the names he used in the film including Wolfgang Preiss, Gert Frobe and Peter van Eyck, many of whom were recognisable for their parts in other Second World War films. However, for the first time, rather than bit parts with characters given little to do, these actors had fair-sized parts that allowed them to show that the German's too were competent in battle. The film is long – at three hours – but remains a staple of the war film genre.

The Green Berets (1968)

FACTS

Released:	19 June 1968
Directed by:	John Wayne
Produced by:	Michael Wayne
Written by:	Robin Moore
Screenplay by:	James Lee Barrett
Starring:	John Wayne, David Janssen, Jim Hutton, Aldo Ray, Mike Henry, George Takei, Luke Askew
Music by:	Miklos Rozsa
Distributed by:	Warner Bros/Seven Arts

■ **BELOW:** John Wayne looks through the film camera to check the next set-up during filming of *The Green Berets*, in which he is both star and director.

The Green Berets was produced at the height of the United States' involvement in the Vietnam War in 1968. With a growing anti-war atmosphere in America, Wayne decided to direct and star in this movie, with presidential approval, in order to counter social discontent. It was well documented that the government wished for actors to keep on making war films (and other genres) in order to boost morale, and while he may not have fought for real, Wayne was perfectly placed to provide the action for the movie theatres. However, it was to become one of the most controversial films that Wayne ever made. By making the film, many believed that Wayne was in support of the war in Vietnam, but more likely was his support of America against Communism. He felt that US politicians were taking a half-hearted approach to Vietnam and he wanted to make a propaganda film about why American troops were in Asia; the movie was considered simple. Wayne was "roasted" by the critics, but the public accepted the film and in its first three months, despite negative feelings about the war, all costs were recouped.

■ **RIGHT:** John Wayne during a visit to US Army Special Forces facilities, Japan. He was looking for possible sites for *The Green Berets*.

22

Hellfighters, about a group of oil well fire-fighters, was quite negatively received with lacklustre reviews and fairly bad ratings. It was described as dull, slow moving, talkative and badly plotted, although other reviews maintained that both Wayne and the director kept a welcome sense of humour. The Duke plays the head of a Houston oil fire-fighting unit who travels around the world putting out dangerous blazes at well heads caused by industrial accidents, explosions or terrorist attacks. The character enjoys his work, but badly misses his ex-wife and daughter who left because she could not bear to see him risk his life any longer. It's been 20 years when Chance Buckman (Wayne) suffers a near-fatal accident, which reunites him with his daughter (Ross). His daughter then marries his right-hand man and Chance takes a safer job in the hope that he can reunite with his ex-wife (Miles). He gives his own company to his new son-in-law as a wedding present. Wayne's character becomes bored of his new executive life and longs to be back in the field so he goes to his son-in-law's aid at an oil well fire in Venezuela, followed unbeknown to him by his wife and daughter. All ends well.

Hellfighters (1968)

FACTS

Released:	27 November 1968
Directed by:	Andrew V McLaglen
Produced by:	Robert Arthur
Written by:	Clair Huffaker
Starring:	John Wayne, Katherine Ross, Jim Hutton, Vera Miles, Jay C Flippen
Music by:	Leonard Rosenman
Distributed by:	Universal Studios

23

■ **RIGHT: Katherine Ross.**

him to track down hired hand, Tom Chaney (Corey), who is responsible for the murder but has fled with "Lucky" Ned Pepper (Duvall), a gang leader whom was once shot by Rooster in a gunfight. Mattie heads off with Rooster into Indian territory and they're joined by a young Texas Ranger who is also looking for Chaney who allegedly also killed a Texas Senator. After quite a bit of action, Chaney is eventually caught, Rooster receives his reward money and is seen riding off into the distance as the film ends. Mia Farrow had been cast to play Mattie, but eventually turned the part down when producer, Wallis, refused to replace director Hathaway with Roman Polanski. Farrow had been warned that the director was far too moody.

Wayne received the Oscar for Best Actor for this film. The film also received nominations for Best Song by Elmer Bernstein, the renowned Hollywood composer, for both Academy and Golden Globe awards. Wayne's character, US Marshal Reuben "Rooster" J Cogburn is hired by 14-year-old Mattie Ross (Darby) for his "true grit" following her father's murder. She wants

■ **ABOVE & BELOW: John Wayne appears to be wiping away a tear from his eye after he was named best actor for his performance in *True Grit*. He is congratulated by actress and singer Barbra Streisand.**

True Grit (1969)

FACTS

Released:	11 June 1969
Directed by:	Henry Hathaway
Produced by:	Hal B Wallis
Written by:	Charles Portis
Screenplay by:	Marguerite Roberts
Starring:	John Wayne, Glen Campbell, Dennis Hopper, Robert Duvall, Kim Darby, Jeff Corey, Strother Martin, John Fiedler
Music by:	Elmer Bernstein
Distributed by:	Paramount Pictures

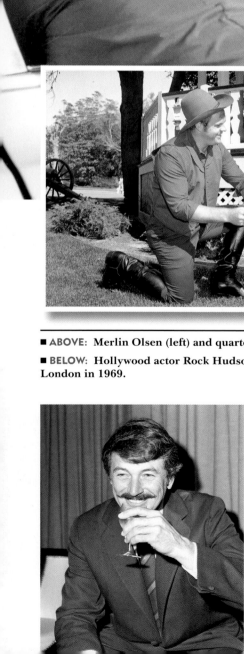

JOHN WAYNE

■ **LEFT:** John Wayne leans out from a car window in Mexico in 1969.

The Undefeated was the first and only time that two Hollywood legends worked together. Wayne and Rock Hudson were both screen icons at the time of production and both were at the height of their popularity and, while the Duke remained in films, Hudson went on to become a leading TV actor during the 1970s, particularly in NBC's *McMillan and Wife*. This Western portrays the events around the French Intervention in Mexico where the plot opens following the American Civil War. Wayne plays Union Colonel, John Henry Thomas, whose company attack a group of Confederate soldiers while not knowing that the war has ended. Led by Colonel James Langdon (Hudson), the Confederate soldiers are preparing to join Emperor Maximilian of Mexico and on 4th July, both sides meet in a drunken brawl while Langdon's daughter and Thomas's son, an adopted Indian by the name of Blue Boy, fall in love. The soldiers go their separate ways but soon meet up again when Langdon's men are held by Mexican Republican General Rojas, and the Union soldiers come to their rescue.

■ **ABOVE:** Merlin Olsen (left) and quarterback Roman Gabriel, both of the Los Angeles Rams, appearing in *The Undefeated*.

■ **BELOW:** Hollywood actor Rock Hudson sips a drink during a press conference held in his honour at the Savoy Hotel in London in 1969.

The Undefeated (1969)

FACTS

Released:	27 November 1969
Directed by:	Andrew V McLaglen (John Wayne – uncredited)
Produced by:	Robert L Jacks
Written by:	James Lee Barrett
Starring:	John Wayne, Rock Hudson
Music by:	Hugo Montenegro
Distributed by:	20th Century Fox

This Technicolor, Warner Bros' Western, saw President Richard Nixon use the film to comment on his views on law and order at a press conference in August 1970. Historically, it was fairly inaccurate with regard to its portrayal of the Lincoln County War in 1878, involving Billy the Kid and Pat Garrett, but as a motion picture it is based loosely on the short story by Fenady, entitled *Chisum and the Lincoln County Cattle War*. Wayne's son Michael decided to produce the movie after he decided that the basic story summed up his father's political beliefs. A good cast was assembled consisting of film friends and recognisable faces for filming in Durango, Mexico. During filming, Wayne was introduced to patriotic poetry by Robert Mitchum's brother, John. Great friend, Tucker, suggested that the two men collaborate on a recording of some of the prose and the album, *America: Why I Love Her*, was born. The spoken album went on to become Grammy-nominated and became a hit again in 2001 following the 9/11 attacks.

■ **LEFT:** Billy the Kid, western outlaw of the late 19th Century, also known as William Bonney.

■ **BELOW:** President Nixon at his White House desk in 1970 after making an appearance on nationwide television.

Chisum (1970)

FACTS

Released:	29 July 1970
Directed by:	Andrew V McLaglen
Produced by:	Andrew J Fenady
Executive Producer:	Michael Wayne
Written by:	Andrew J Fenady
Narrated by:	William Conrad
Starring:	John Wayne, Forrest Tucker, Geoffrey Deuel, Ben Johnson
Music by:	Dominic Frontiere
Distributed by:	Warner Bros

■ **ABOVE:** John Wayne, nominated by the Motion Picture Academy for best actor for his performance in *True Grit*, arrives at the Music Center in Los Angeles.

In this sequel to 1969's *True Grit,* Wayne's character, Rooster Cogburn makes a comeback as the questionable US Marshal. Now stripped of his badge due to his use of firearms and drunkenness, the aging Cogburn is given a second chance when a gang of violent, ruthless killers murder an elderly preacher and commit other crimes in a village within Indian territory. The preacher's daughter, Eula Goodnight, enlists the unwilling Rooster to help track down the gang who have gone on the run with a shipment of nitroglycerin, which they've stolen. It was the only time that Wayne appeared opposite Katharine Hepburn in a movie. The film was shot on location in Deschutes County, Oregon for the mountain scenes and on the Deschutes River for the rapids. Further river scenes were filmed on location on the Rogue River while other shots came from Smith Rock State

Park. Producer, Wallis worked with his wife, Martha Hyer, for this production, which was poorly received by the critics. It became a moderate hit at the box office and was expected to follow with a further film also starring Wayne as Rooster, but plans were scrapped when the Hollywood legend eventually died of cancer in 1979 (although a low-budget TV version was released in 1978 starring another actor, Warren Oates). Wayne only made one more film following *Rooster Cogburn* in 1976 entitled *The Shootist.*

■ **ABOVE:** Katharine Hepburn.

Rooster Cogburn (1975)

FACTS

Released:	17 October 1975
Directed by:	Stuart Millar
Produced by:	Paul Nathan, Hal B Wallis
Written by:	Martha Hyer, Charles Portis
Starring:	John Wayne, Katharine Hepburn
Music by:	Laurence Rosenthal
Distributed by:	Universal Pictures

Chapter 2

In Private

■ **ABOVE:** The birthplace of Marion Robert Morrison.

John Wayne was the Duke's stage name and he was born Marion Robert Morrison (later changed to Marion Mitchell Morrison) on 26 May 1907 at 216 South Second Street in Winterset, Iowa to Clyde Leonard Morrison (1884-1937) and Mary "Molly" Alberta Brown (1885-1970). He weighed around 13 pounds, establishing from the very beginning that he was going to have a huge presence in life. His middle name was changed to Mitchell – like his grandfather's – when his parents decided to name their second son Robert. The family were of Scots-Irish descent on both sides and Wayne was brought up a Presbyterian. He soon decided that he preferred being called "Little" Duke rather

than Marion after the family's Airedale Terrier, Duke, (the dog was known as "Big" Duke) and the name seemed to stick. When Wayne's family moved to Glendale California (1911) after a few years in Lancester, where his father failed to find success as a farmer, he eventually went to Wilson Middle School in Glendale where he discovered he had a talent for sports. He played football for the Glendale High School team champions in 1924 but went on to study law at the University of Southern California (USC) in 1925, having been rejected by the US Naval Academy. He played for the university football team, but injury would bring his sporting and

academic career to an end. The injury was sustained while body surfing and he desperately tried to hide his suffering from the football coaches as without the athletic scholarship he'd gained, Wayne was unable to fund his academic studies. As a youngster, he'd sold ice creams for a man who shod horses for Hollywood studios and it was this connection that saw him begin working at local film studios once his time at USO came to an end. Tom Mix, a leading Hollywood silent actor, put Wayne forward for a job in the prop department in exchange for football tickets and Duke Morrison began his transformation to John Wayne, the actor, director and producer who would become

■ **ABOVE:** **Hollywood Western film actor Tom Mix and his horse Tony perform a stunt in 1923.**

the biggest box-office draw of all time. (Even today, John Wayne is a bigger star the world over than the likes of George Clooney, Brad Pitt and Morgan Freeman.)

Slowly but surely Wayne began to gain bit parts – in the name of Duke Morrison – and established a life-long friendship with renowned director, John

Ford. "John Wayne" was "born" when director, Raoul Walsh, saw him working as a prop boy and wanted to give him a role in his 1930 film, *The Big Trail*. Anthony

■ **ABOVE: Film director John Ford.**

Wayne was a serious suggestion, but after further discussion the first name John was muted and agreed. Duke had around 10 years acting in B-movies until he got his big break with *Stagecoach* in 1939, but during this time he began developing his on-screen persona; the man of action, the hero, romantic and all-round American, the swagger and the calming drawl which would make him a household name and lead him to one of the most enduring careers in Hollywood. It was planned, it was executed, and according to the big man himself (he was 6 foot 4 inches) it was practiced, and for generations of Wayne fans, it worked.

While his film career continued to grow, with inevitable ups and downs, including the rise of the "talkie" and the commercial flop of Walsh's film, Wayne's private life was equally complex. He would marry three times, and despite being accused of being racist, all the Duke's marriages were to ladies from Latin America. His first wife, whom he married in 1933, was Josephine Alicia Saenz with whom he had four children: Michael Wayne – the producer – (1934-2003), Mary Antonia "Toni" Wayne LaCava (1936-2000), Patrick Wayne – an actor – (born 1939) and Melinda Wayne Munoz (born 1940). But the marriage was not to last (it ended in 1945) and he married his second wife, Esperanza Baur Diaz. Wayne met Diaz (nicknamed "Chata") while on holiday in Mexico and they married in 1946. The union, unlike his first marriage (Josephine, daughter of a Panamian Consul, had disliked the Hollywood film world), was rocky from the start. The couple ended their relationship when the former actress from Mexico became convinced that Wayne was having an affair with one of his co-stars, Gail Russell. He denied the affair. As Wayne returned home from an after-filming party, his extremely drunken wife tried to shoot him for his alleged infidelity. This marriage too ended in divorce (in 1953), and his third wife, Pilar Pallete Weldy, the daughter of a Peruvian politician, gave him three more children: Aissa Wayne (born 1956), John Ethan Wayne – also an actor – (born 1962) and Marisa Wayne (born 1966). But Wayne did have a number of high-profile affairs. His extra-marital relationship with Marlene Dietrich lasted for three years after the pair met on set in 1940 and made two further films together. They remained friends even after their affair ended. Eventually Wayne's third marriage began to crumble. Many in Hollywood were surprised that Duke had

■ **ABOVE:** The marriage certificate of Marion Morrison and Josephine Saenz.
■ **BELOW RIGHT:** Michael Wayne (left) and Patrick Wayne, sons of John Wayne, attending the John Wayne Cancer Institute.
■ **BELOW:** Gail Russell.

married three Latin-American women; it was according to reports, the only "un-American" thing about him. Wayne described this as coincidental and that whenever he had time off, he happened to be in South America at the time. He claimed that he had nothing against American women, but that Latin-American women seemed to dress more for their men, simple and understated, while American women dressed more for each other. He didn't care for

jewellery and detested "flashy". He is described as a gentle man, one who actually enjoyed domesticity and sentimentality. Wayne enjoyed family birthdays – he never forgot one – and liked to select dresses for his wives to wear. He even enjoyed shopping, but most of all, when he wasn't working, Duke liked to spend time with his children and he adored them all. Much later, he became romantically involved for seven years with Pat Stacy who landed a job as his secretary when her former boss moved to Chicago. He was a tax advisor to the stars and offered her the chance to work with one of the biggest and the best because Mary St John was retiring as the Duke's secretary. Stacy didn't want to move to Chicago, but didn't really know much about Hollywood either. St John interviewed Stacy at length and offered her the job there and then, working at Wayne's production company, Batjac, situated in Paramount

■ **ABOVE:** John Wayne finds he can play in pictures and satisfy his love for chess almost at the same time. When he has a few minutes to idle he engages Marlene Dietrich in a game. Both are making the film, *Pittsburgh*.

■ **LEFT:** John Wayne testifies from the witness stand in a Los Angeles court room during his alimony fight with his estranged wife Esperanza Bauer Diaz, in 1953.

■ **BELOW:** John Wayne is seen at the Hampshire House in New York after learning he was voted "King of the Box Office" in 1955.

■ **LEFT:** John Wayne is shown prior to leaving Good Samaritan Hospital in Los Angeles, on 7 October 1964. Wayne was hospitalised for two weeks and underwent two operations.

■ **RIGHT:** John Wayne, making his first movie since his operation for cancer, lines up for lunch filming *The Sons of Katie Elder*.

Studios. It was three weeks after Stacy took the job before she met Wayne who insisted that she call him Duke. Their romance didn't begin until Wayne's third marriage was over and Pilar had left him for good, but Stacy provided the man she considered warm and compassionate with companionship for the final years of his life.

Stacy had been surprised when she first met Wayne that he wore a hairpiece, but Duke's hair had been thinning since the 1940s and he'd taken to wearing one since that time, although did occasionally go out without a toupee. He wasn't worried that people knew. He was a grounded, solid character with a likeable personality and a great sense of humour, but like all people, had his faults. It was well known that directors were keen to ensure that Wayne's scenes were filmed before lunch. The afternoon would be too late as Duke would be drunk and was often described as "a mean drunk". He was widely known for his heavy drinking and chain-smoking cigarettes (he smoked up to six packets a day) and was first diagnosed with cancer in 1964; this led to surgery to remove his left lung and several ribs. He was advised to keep his condition quiet – for fear of losing work – but Wayne did quite the opposite and made his cancer extremely public so that his audiences the world over would think about their lives and make sure they were checked by a doctor should they have any concerns of their own. Within five years he was cancer free, but the loss of his lung affected his ability to work for long hours and he often required oxygen to aid his breathing. Duke had given up smoking by this time, but slowly and surely, from beginning to chew tobacco he was back in the habit – this time, however, it was cigars and they remained a constant companion until the time of his death.

Wayne had been involved with the Freemasons since his youth and was a member of a number of Lodges. He'd first become involved with the organisation when he joined the Order of DeMolay, a youth group associated with the Masons, where he was an active member. In his later years, he invested in an oil company and a shrimp business in Panama and even bought the island of Taborcillo just off the main coast (which was sold from his estate after his death). He also owned cattle ranches in Stanfield and Springerville in Arizona and a 135-foot yacht, although he did become more conservative in his financial dealings towards the end of his life.

Duke moved to Orange County in California in the 1960s where he remained a prominent Republican in Hollywood. Wayne was diagnosed with cancer again (this time of the stomach) in 1978. He had enrolled on a cancer vaccine study in order to keep cancer at bay, but he died of the disease at the UCLA Medical Center on 11 June 1979. His grave at the Pacific View Memorial Park cemetery remained unmarked for 20 years until his family agreed to use a quotation

Wayne had once used in an interview. It reads: "Tomorrow is the most important thing in life. Comes into us at midnight very clean. It's perfect when it arrives and it puts itself in our hands. It hopes we've learned something from yesterday".

■ ABOVE: John Wayne at the 51ˢᵗ Annual Academy Awards in Hollywood, 1979. Wayne, who had cancer, was making his first public appearance since he underwent surgery in January.

■ BELOW: UCLA Medical Center administrator Bernard Strohm announces the death of actor John Wayne in Los Angeles, 11 June 1979. Strohm said Wayne had been in a coma for 24 hours before his death at 5.30pm.

Chapter 3:
Leading Ladies and Supporting Men

■ **ABOVE:** Jimmy Stewart explains things to Donna Reed in *It's a Wonderful Life.*

John Wayne deplored truly violent or "close to the edge movies" such as *Rosemary's Baby* 1968, and liked films to contain some romance. He may have played a "part" many times over, but he was working to a well-oiled formula that saw him star successfully with some of the other Hollywood greats including Maureen O'Hara, Ward Bond, Jim Hutton, Bruce Cabot, Ben Johnson, Edward Faulkner, Jay C Flippen, Richard Boone, Chuck Roberson, Claire Trevor, Marlene Dietrich, Susan Hayward, Angie Dickinson, Capucine, Elsa Martinelli, Donna Reed, Martha Hyer, Patricia Neal, Colleen Dewhurst, Lauren Bacall and Katharine Hepburn to name but a few. Within the films he chose, Wayne was always a genuine American hero, which at the time of his greatest achievements, worked well with the ideals of the American people while symbolising the essence of the country's soul. He wasn't the only hero: there was Fonda,

Stewart and Cooper, of course, while amongst the ladies there were very few; it seemed that patriotism could only be attributed to leading men.

Henry Fonda was often personified on screen as the farmer-pioneer and in fact debuted in the movies with *The Farmer Takes a Wife* in 1935. The film was a romantic drama set a decade before where a down-to-earth man farming the land wishes for nothing more than to be happy working alongside his loyal wife. He later starred in *The Grapes of Wrath*, which is muted as his finest performance for Hollywood, while other roles came with *Drums Along the Mohawk, Mister Roberts* – where he played an American soldier – and *Twelve Angry Men*.

Jimmy Stewart was another all-American hero who also starred alongside Wayne. Known for his "small-town lawyer" roles, Stewart was often found in Frank Capra films where he played an ordinary man going about an ordinary existence. It was another form of heroic idealism amongst American audiences including *The American Dream* and *Mr Smith Goes to Washington*. He played a young sheriff in *Destiny Rides Again*, where he proved that despite appearances, he was more than capable of showing grit and determination within the roles he chose when he needed to. One of his most well-loved roles, again with Capra, came as George Bailey in *It's a Wonderful Life* where the character actually tries to break away from a small-town image destined for better things, only to find that his original status is what makes

■ **LEFT: Henry Fonda dressed for his part in *Mister Roberts*.**

■ **ABOVE:** John Wayne is seen with fellow actors, Irene Dunne (left), Rosalind Russell and Jimmy Stewart at the premiere of *How The West Was Won.*

■ **RIGHT:** Film fisticuffs always appear so real and deadly but the roundhouse right James Stewart is throwing to John Wayne looks like the perfect form for a perfect punch, in fact, Stewart missed him by a mile. This is the way director John Ford staged it for the production of *The Man Who Shot Liberty Valance.* To screen audiences, however, it looked as if Stewart connected squarely on Wayne's jaw.

him truly happy. He showed his true stardom in *The Stratton Story* as a hero of baseball with an artificial limb, and *The Glenn Miller Story*, where the films were of a biographical nature. Wayne didn't play as many real-life heroes as Stewart, nor did he opt for biographical films as a genre, although he did play Frank "Spig" Wead, a Navy Aviation Commander who went on to become a successful Hollywood screenwriter, in the movie *Wings of the Eagle*, directed by Ford, while for John Huston he portrayed Townsend Harris, the first American ambassador to Japan in *The Barbarian and the Geisha.* And, then of course, there was Davy Crockett in *The Alamo*, which despite all the criticism, he took great pride in.

Amongst Wayne's leading ladies, Maureen O'Hara was one of his favourites. As already mentioned in the film section, the chemistry between these two Hollywood stars was electric with its "push me, pull me" tension and the two actors became close friends. The couple were

■ **ABOVE:** *The Alamo,* **directed by John Wayne who also starred in the film as Davy Crockett.**

■ **RIGHT:** **Maureen O'Hara, clad in pantaloons, swings over John Wayne in a scene from** *McLintock.*

more like brother and sister in their approach and had great respect for each other. Wayne undoubtedly had sex appeal, without it he wouldn't have become the leading man he did, however heroic he came across. His appeal was shaped, defined and recognised, in part, by the leading ladies he worked with and O'Hara was no exception. However, many of the actors working with Wayne were not the stereotypical sex goddesses that it may be imagined he would play opposite. Claire Trevor was one of the first actors to work regularly with Wayne. She starred in *Stagecoach*, *Allegheny Uprising* and *Dark Command* with Duke, but is probably better remembered (at least for her films with Wayne) for being his leading lady at the time he made his breakthrough than for her sex appeal, despite the fact she undoubtedly had it. Then there was Marlene Dietrich,

who at the time she met Wayne, had the pick of Hollywood for any leading man she chose. She first met with Wayne in a Hollywood canteen and demanded that he play opposite her. Wayne, for his part, proved a worthy actor in *Seven Sinners, The Spoilers* and *Pittsburgh*. The fact that Dietrich was a strong woman on screen with a commanding presence was endearing against Wayne's slightly awkward man persona. But Wayne wasn't always successful with his leading ladies. The three films he made with Susan Hayward seemed to have no sexual chemistry and did little to promote either actor, although both went on to become huge stars. It was with O'Hara that he found the sexual chemistry audiences were clamouring for. He was also cast alongside Angie Dickinson, Elsa Martinelli, Donna Reed and Martha Hyer during the middle phase of his

career when Wayne's sex appeal was still very much in evidence. But, he continued to exude that special something into his later roles when he starred with the likes of Patricia Neal in *In Harm's Way*, and Lauren Bacall in *The Shootist*. Other roles saw him opposite Colleen Dewhurt and, of course, Katharine Hepburn. It was somehow as if the stronger and more intelligent the actress,

■ **LEFT:** John Wayne does his own stunt in a scene with co-star Maureen O'Hara, in the 1963 movie *McLintock*.

■ **RIGHT:** Baseball great Babe Ruth is signing a baseball for actress Claire Trevor.

■ **BELOW:** Marlene Dietrich puts on a few finishing touches for her role as a saloon owner in the film *The Spoilers*. John Wayne, Marlene's leading man, looks on.

the more powerful and heroic Wayne became. The leading ladies in his career certainly added to the special qualities that Wayne portrayed on screen and allowed his characters – and screen persona – to flourish. Of all his leading ladies, none were the typical glamour queens that Hollywood had become accustomed to. However, they commanded attention with their dynamic screen presences and helped propel Wayne yet further up the sexual stakes. There were critics that thought his later roles – despite the fact he shied away from playing opposite women too young for him – were somewhat ridiculous, but for others, Wayne still possessed a sexual range far beyond that of his younger contemporaries. For many generations of fans, his on-screen presence and persona lasted from beginning to end and despite the fact it's more than 30 years since he died, his continued popularity seemingly show that John Wayne's movies look set to do that for some considerable time to come.

■ **RIGHT:** Italian screen actress Sophia Loren and John Wayne relax in the ruins of an old Roman city near Tripoli, Libya in 1957, during a break in the filming of *The Legend of the Lost* on location in the Libyan desert. Wayne plays the desert guide.

■ **BELOW:** Actor Ronald Reagan with Patricia Neal, his co-star in the film *The Hasty Heart*, leaving Waterloo Station, London.

Chapter 4:
Politics, Views and Influences

John Wayne had no interest in politics in his younger years – fellow actor Henry Fonda even went so far as to say "When we first made movies together, the Duke couldn't even spell politics" – and it wasn't until he was elected to the board of the Screen Actors' Guild in the 1940s that he began to be more aware of people's differing views on potentially sensitive and explosive issues. By the mid-1940s, he had helped to found the Motion Picture Alliance for the Preservation of American Ideals, with Walt Disney and movie directors Leo McCarey and Sam Wood, with fellow members including Ward Bond, Gary Cooper and Ronald Reagan. In its ideals they emphasised their resentment to "the growing impression that this industry is made of, and dominated by, Communists, radicals and crackpots."

Wayne, an ardent anti-Communist, served three terms as president (from 1949 until 1952) at a time when Senator Joseph McCarthy and his HUAC were on a witch-hunt for thousands of Americans who were accused of being Communists or communist sympathisers. This encompassed many screenwriters, actors, directors, musicians and other US entertainment professionals who were denied employment in the field because of their political beliefs or associations…

real or suspected! A supporter of McCarthy's unorthodox policy, Wayne – who classed McCarthy as a close friend and about whom he said "I admired the work he did. Whether he went overboard or not, he was of value to my country" – made the movie *Big Jim McLain* in 1951 in which he and James Arness played HUAC investigators taking on Communists in Hawaii.

Despite being warned by studio executives that such a connection would have a detrimental effect on his career in terms of box-office success, the Duke was the top attraction as the 1950s began and, of course, he is not the only actor to become involved in politics. He was one of the few, however, who was able to successfully merge his political and acting careers and

■ BELOW: Senator Joseph McCarthy poses with his article in *Cosmopolitan* in Washington 24 April 1952, in which he repeats some of the charges he made in congress, under immunity, re Communists in government.

■ **LEFT:** After finishing their testimony before the House Un-American Activities Committee in Washington 23 October 1947, film actors pose for photographers with the Capitol Dome in the background. From left to right: Robert Montgomery, George Murphy and Ronald Reagan. They gave investigators testimony on Communism in Hollywood.

Communists to the Nazis: "We were on foreign territory too when we joined Britain to push back Hitler and crush the evil of Nazism... We fought in Germany because of what they were doing to the Jews and to freedom, and as far as I'm concerned the Communists are the enemy, not the Russian or Chinese people". His view had mellowed by 1970 though, as he explained "Communism is still quite obviously a threat yet they are human beings, with a right to their point of view".

Despite avoiding political topics when appearing on talk shows, Wayne had been one of the Republicans' most visible supporters since the 1950s, backing Eisenhower's presidential campaigns in 1952 and 1956. He also supported Richard

his 1968 offering *The Green Berets* did not meet with the unanimous disapproval that many thought it should with its pro-Vietnam sentiments. A June 1966 trip to cheer American troops had left him angry to "see our boys there getting killed and maimed and people back home aren't behind them".

He also justified America's involvement by comparing

■ **BELOW:** US presidential candidate and former Alabama Governor George Wallace.

Nixon in 1960, 1968 and 1972 although preferred to provide his assistance in vocal and monetary terms rather than as a participant. George Wallace considered Wayne as his vice-presidential candidate in 1968 while he was also asked to run for national office the same year. The Duke declined both offers, joking that he did not believe the public would seriously consider an actor in the White House! Wayne was unwavering in his support of friend and colleague Ronald Reagan during his rise from Governor of California in 1966 to his presidential campaign of 1976. Sadly, the Duke would not live long enough to see an actor take the helm in the Oval Office...

Despite the public's affection and adulation for John Wayne the movie star, his personal views did at times upset and annoy people. In spite of the fact that all three of his wives were of Latin descent, he was accused on several occasions of being a racist and appeared to support the notion of white supremacy in America.

"When we came to America," he stated, "there were a few thousand Indians over millions of miles, and I don't feel we did anything wrong in taking this great country away from these people, taking their happy hunting grounds away. There were great numbers of people who needed new land and the Indians were selfishly trying to keep it for themselves."

He was criticised by both Native and African Americans but protested that he had always portrayed Native Americans as proud, courageous and dignified people in his films. He defended his record with black actors explaining that he had a black slave in *The Alamo* and a proportionally correct number of black actors in *The Green Berets* although it was pointed out that around 25 per cent of working cowboys in the 19th Century were black.

Thankfully for his millions of fans, John Wayne's often-controversial views did not rein in his onscreen adventures. It might have been a different story, however, if Joseph Stalin's order

50

JOHN WAYNE

had been successfully carried out. The Soviet Union Premier (from 1941 until 1952) was a movie buff who was so incensed with Wayne's anti-Communism that he ordered his assassination but died before it could be implemented. When successor Nikita Khrushchev met Wayne in 1958, he explained that he had rescinded the instruction but how different would life on the silver screen have been if they had succeeded...

■ **BELOW:** President Ford and John Wayne move through a crowd estimated at 23,000 at Fountain Valley, California, 24 October 1976.

Chapter 5:
Awards, Honours and Trademarks

Swagger

1   *A slight or moderate exaggeration in the side-to-side movements of walking.*
2   *A usually masculine style of upper-body strutting.*
3   *A visual means of filling-up space or occupying a greater expanse of personal territory.*

John Wayne became synonymous with American culture and its values during the 20th Century. A full 50 years of screen appearances led to him being widely regarded as an enduring all-American hero who epitomised rugged masculinity, and his popularity shows no sign of waning more than 30 years after his death. Indeed, it is still possible to buy replicas of the actor's hats, guns and holsters online as the 21st Century enters its second decade. Wayne's physical presence was combined with a distinctive voice and walk that established him as one of the greatest movie icons of all time, yet fame didn't come instantly.

Lifelong friend and fellow actor Paul Fix (1901-1983) has been credited with teaching Wayne his "rolling walk" as the youngster was just beginning his career. Wayne allegedly wanted a trait that set him apart from his contemporaries, and Fix – who went on to become a household name in the 1958 TV series *The Rifleman* – suggested that he adopt the rolling gait that went on to become his trademark.

By the time he filmed *Stagecoach* in 1939, the Duke had already mastered his

distinctive method of delivering his lines with a stop-start speech pattern that would go on to win him millions of fans. He had also mastered his unique swagger

(that many have tried but failed to emulate) and the first pairing of Wayne with director John Ford would catapult the former Marion Morrison to international stardom.

A succession of leading ladies starred opposite but Wayne was struggling with his weight by the 1950s and, at the age of 51, he believed that he was too old to be cast as the romantic lead. His solution was to revert to playing "John Wayne" in each of his films, although 1960's *North To Alaska* did showcase his comedic talents. Wayne was also very careful at selecting roles that would not compromise his off-screen image, and ordered a rewrite of the script for his final

■ **ABOVE: Paul Fix.**
■ **RIGHT: Maureen O'Hara and John Wayne during filming of *McLintock*.**

film *The Shootist* (1976) because he refused to allow his character to shoot someone in the back.

With a career spanning so many decades and films, it was inevitable that John Wayne was awarded numerous accolades. Here are a few highlights:

• He became the 125th star to have his hands and feet immortalised outside Grauman's Chinese Theatre on the Hollywood Walk of Fame in January 1950. The sand used in the cement was brought all the way from Iwo Jima in honour of his 1949 film.

• He was nominated for the Best Actor in a Leading Role Oscar for *Sands Of Iwo Jima* in 1949 but lost out to Broderick Crawford with *All The King's Men*. Wayne himself often stated that he wished his first Oscar nomination had been for *She Wore A Yellow Ribbon* but it was not to be.

• His second Oscar nomination came in the Best Picture category for *The Alamo* in 1960. This time he lost out to *The Apartment*, produced by Billy Wilder.

• He was voted Star of the Decade 1950-60 by the *Motion Picture Herald*, the American film industry trade paper published from 1931 to December 1972.

• He was awarded the Cecil B DeMille Award in 1966 for outstanding contributions to the world of entertainment by the Hollywood Foreign Press Association.

• He finally won his only Oscar in 1969 for his portrayal of Rooster Cogburn in *True Grit*. This was seen by many to be in recognition of his lifetime achievement, with his performance being widely

■ **BELOW: A Japanese noodleman carrying noodles on his shoulder rides past 75ft-high John Wayne on a horse publicising** *The Alamo*, **which plays to a capacity crowd everyday at the Pantheon Theater in Tokyo, Japan, in July 1961.**

54

■ **ABOVE: Ronald Reagan shakes hands with President Jimmy Carter.**

■ **ABOVE LEFT: The Olympic Torch at the east end of the Los Angeles Memorial Coliseum burns in tribute to honour John Wayne. The torch was erected in 1932 when Los Angeles hosted the Olympic Games for that year.**

■ **LEFT: A Madame Tussaud wax work of John Wayne.**

criticised, although actor-turned-politician Ronald Reagan later wrote that he believed it was as recompense for Wayne not receiving earlier nominations for *Red River* (1948), *She Wore A Yellow Ribbon* (1949) and *The Searchers* (1956). Having been presented with his Oscar, Wayne allegedly told Richard Burton that he should have won it instead for his performance in *Anne Of A Thousand Days*.

- In 1973 he was awarded The National Americanism Gold Medal, the Veteran of Foreign Wars' highest accolade. The same year saw him awarded the Gold Medal from the National Football Foundation for his days playing football for Glendale High School and USC.
- He was inducted into the Hall of Great Western Performers of the National Cowboy and Western Heritage Museum in 1974.
- He won the People's Choice Award for most popular motion picture actor each year between 1975 and 1978.
- He was awarded the Congressional Gold Medal on 26 May 1979 with the simple inscription reading "John Wayne, American".
- The Olympic Torch flame in Los Angeles' Coliseum was lit on 11 June 1979 to honour his memory and remained alight until his funeral four days later.
- President Jimmy Carter posthumously awarded Wayne the nation's highest civilian award – the Presidential Medal of Freedom – on 9 June 1980.
- Sculptor Robert Summers was commissioned to create a nine-foot bronze statue of the Duke to welcome passengers to the John Wayne Airport in Orange County.
- He was named America's Favourite Movie Star in a Harris Poll conducted in 1995. He has appeared in every annual Top 10 since 1994 and was still ranked as third on the list in January 2011, the only deceased star to make the grade.
- Arnold Schwarzenegger, as Governor of California, proclaimed that 26 May 2007 – the centennial of Wayne's birth – was "John Wayne Day".

Chapter 6:
Trivia and Quotes

Trivia

- John Wayne made several appearances as a singing cowboy early in his career. Despite allegedly having a rich baritone singing voice, Wayne's vocals were overdubbed by Smith Ballew who was standing out of the camera's range of vision.

- Wayne was particularly keen on the role of Buffalo Bill in Cecil B DeMille's 1936 film *The Plainsman* because he thought it would make him a star, but the director chose Gary Cooper instead.

- Wayne was in line for the lead role in *The Gunfighter* (1950) after Harry Cohn – president and production director of Columbia Pictures – bought the story intending to star the Duke as Jimmy Ringo. It turned pear-shaped, however, when Wayne refused to work for Cohn (who had mistreated him at the beginning of his acting career) so the project was sold to 20th Century Fox.

- John Wayne's favourite film was *The Searchers* (1956) and he named his son Ethan in honour of his role in what went on to be named the Greatest American Western of all time by the American Film Institute in 2008.

- Suffering from thinning hair towards the end of the 1940s, John Wayne wore a toupee in every film from *Wake Of The Red Witch* (1948) onwards, although he would remove it in order to portray his characters

SUCCESSFULLY INTRODUCED BY
SMITH BALLEW

■ **ABOVE: Smith Ballew.**

getting older. He was rarely seen without his trademark hairpiece although he was "natural" when attending Gary Cooper's funeral in May 1961. During a widely noted appearance at Harvard University, Wayne was asked by a student, "Where did you get that phony hair?" to which he responded, "It's not phony. It's real hair. Of course, it's not mine, but it's real."

- Wayne bought a former minesweeper in 1962 and christened the 135-foot yacht *The Wild Goose*. He chipped ice from an iceberg during one of his voyages and would frequently add this to his favourite drink, Sauza Conmemorativo Tequila. It was alleged that Wayne only agreed to star in the film *Circus World*

(1964) so that he could have the enjoyment of sailing his yacht to Europe.

- Wayne was forced to rely heavily on an oxygen mask following the removal of a lung in 1964 and an oxygen tank was always on hand during filming. This proved problematic when flying and while filming *True Grit* (1969) and *Rooster Cogburn* (1975) due to the high altitude of the films' locations. It was stipulated, however, that the press were not allowed to take any photograph of the screen legend breathing through his mask.

- Newspaper reports in June 1966 suggested that John Wayne had almost been killed following a sniper attack during a visit to troops serving in Vietnam. What they didn't make clear was that while the sniper's bullet had struck the Duke's bicycle, the movie icon was nowhere near at the time.

- Wayne underwent plastic surgery in 1969 when the crow lines around his eyes were removed. The operation left him with two black eyes and he wore dark glasses for a fortnight until he had healed. The star also had surgery to remove his jowls.

- Wayne allegedly turned down the lead in the crime thriller *Dirty Harry* (1971) because he felt that the role of unorthodox policeman Harry Callaghan did not suit his screen image. Ironically, the Duke changed his mind after seeing the genre-defining classic

---

■ **ABOVE RIGHT: Gary Cooper.**

■ **RIGHT: Actors Patrick Wayne (left), and John Ethan Wayne, sons of actor John Wayne, pose for a photo during the United States Postal Service's unveiling of its annual "Legends of Hollywood" commemorative postage stamp in 2004.**

■ **BELOW: Claudia Cardinale (left) with John Wayne and Rita Hayworth, appearing in the film _Circus World_, during shooting on location near Madrid, Spain.**

■ **ABOVE:** John Wayne, making his first visit to London in 10 years, raises his glass as he talks to newsmen at London's Grosvenor Hotel in 1974. He said he was feeling in good health after his recent struggle against cancer which left him with only one lung. "I am still smoking and drinking and standing up to it. I'm feeling pretty good", he said.

and went on to make two police dramas in *McQ* (1974) and *Brannigan* (1975).

- Although the final result was heavily processed, Wayne provided the voice for the character of Imperial Spy Garindan in the first offering of George Lucas' *Star Wars* saga. Simply entitled *Star Wars* when originally released in 1977, it has since been relabelled *Star Wars Episode IV: A New Hope* following the release of the prequel trilogy between 1999 and 2005.

- John Wayne was buried in secret following his death but his grave remained unmarked for 20 years amid fears that Vietnam War protesters might desecrate his final resting place. This was rectified in 1999 when a bronze plaque featuring an image of John Wayne astride a horse near the Alamo was added to the headstone. It had been alleged that Duke wanted a simple epitaph carved on his headstone – "Feo, Fuerte y Formal" meaning "He was Ugly, Strong and had Dignity" – but sadly, his wishes were never carried out.

- Orange County Airport was officially renamed John Wayne Airport following the screen icon's death in 1979. Wayne – who had lived in nearby Newport Beach – became the first entertainer to have an airport named after him.

- John Wayne was honoured with an Army helicopter in May 1998 called *The Duke*. In a naming ceremony in Washington DC attended by some of his family, eldest son Michael stated that his father "loved this country and he loved its traditions".

- During his career, Wayne's movies grossed an estimated

■ **ABOVE: A John Wayne statue.**

half a billion dollars worldwide… a far cry from today's box-office successes such as *Avatar*. James Cameron's 2009 epic creation heads the list of highest grossing movies of all time with takings of more than $2.75 billion.

- Instructions were set out in John Wayne's will that no footage of him smoking should ever be shown again because of his fight against lung cancer.

This proved a hurdle for director Jason Reitman's 2005 project *Thank You For Smoking* and he had to petition the Duke's family to allow them to use footage of Wayne's *Sands Of Iwo Jima* character lighting a cigarette after surviving the battle only to then be killed by a sniper. Thankfully, the family agreed to allow the scene to be included in the comedy drama after they had seen the script.

Quotes

"There's been a lot of stories about how I got to be called Duke. One was that I played the part of a duke in a school play – which I never did. Sometimes, they even said I was descended from royalty! It was all a lot of rubbish. Hell, the truth is that I was named after a dog!"

■ **BELOW:** A publicity shot of John Wayne and Vera Ralston for the 1945 film, *Dakota*.

"If it hadn't been for football and the fact I got my leg broke and had to go into the movies to eat, why, who knows, I mighta turned out to be a Liberal Democrat."

"I don't act... I react."

"Put a man aboard a horse, and right off you've got the makings of something magnificent. Physical strength, speed where you can feel it, plus heroism. And the hero, he's big and strong. You pit another strong man against him, with both their lives at stake, and right there's a simplicity of conflict you just can't beat."

■ **ABOVE:** John Wayne shows Barry White of Clapham how to hold a gun on the five-year-old's birthday, at Granada Cinema in Tooting, London, in 1951.

"Westerns are closer to art than anything else in the motion picture business."

"Those who like me already know me, and those who don't like me wouldn't want to read about me anyway."

"I play John Wayne in every part regardless of the character, and I've been doing okay, haven't I?"

"I've always followed my father's advice: he told me, first to always keep my word and, second, to never insult anybody unintentionally. If I insult you, you can be goddamn sure I intend to. And, third, he told me not to go around looking for trouble."

"You know, I hear everybody talking about the generation gap. Frankly, sometimes I don't know what they're talking about. Heck, by now I should know a little bit about it, if I'm ever going to. I have seven kids and eighteen grandkids and I don't seem to have any trouble

talking to any of them. Never have had, and I don't intend to start now."

"I've always had deep faith that there is a Supreme Being, there has to be. To me that's just a normal thing to have that kind of faith. The fact that He's let me stick around a little longer, or She's let me stick around a little longer, certainly goes great with me – and I want to hang around as long as I'm healthy and not in anybody's way."

■ **RIGHT:** Frank Sinatra and John Wayne get together during an event in Santa Monica, 1965, in a photo taken by Don Pack, Sinatra's personal photographer from 1960 to 1980.

■ **BELOW:** Frank Sinatra (left) and Bob Hope break up over the sight, and sound, of John Wayne, second from left, and Bing Crosby pretending to sing a duet as the four stars prepared to tape a two-hour special, Bob Hope's Quarter-Century of Comedy at NBC in Los Angeles, 16 October 1975.

64